Exploring the Ocean Floor

Heather Rising

Exploring the Ocean Floor

Text: Heather Rising
Publishers: Tania Mazzeo and Eliza Webb
Series consultant: Amanda Sutera
Hands on Heads Consulting
Editor: Susan Keogh
Project editor: Annabel Smith
Designer: Leigh Ashforth
Project designer: Danielle Maccarone
Illustrations: Fabian Slongo
Permissions researcher: Lumina Datamatics
Production controller: Renee Tome

Acknowledgements
We would like to thank the following for permission to reproduce copyright material:

Front cover: TamaraP/Shutterstock.com; p. 4: (top) Rasto SK/Shutterstock.com; (bottom) Natalja Petuhova/Shutterstock.com; p. 5: (top) Ken Griffiths/Shutterstock.com; (bottom) Leah-Anne Thompson/Shutterstock.com; p. 6: Royal Astronomical Society/Science Source; p. 7: (top) Smith Archive/Alamy Stock Photo; p. 8: (bottom) FedBul/Shutterstock.com; p. 9: (top) IanDagnall Computing/Alamy Stock Photo; (bottom) Buzz Pictures/Alamy Stock Photo; p. 11: martin berry/Alamy Stock Photo; p. 12: Jon Davison/Alamy Stock Photo; p. 13: (top) lego 19861111/Shutterstock.com; (bottom) Imeh Akpanudosen/Getty Images Entertainment/Getty Images; p. 14: vanhurck/Shutterstock.com; p. 15: (top) richard sowersby/Alamy Stock Photo; p. 16: Geography Photos/Universal Images Group/Getty Images; p. 17: (top) Ziga Plahutar/Alamy Stock Photo; (bottom left) Teodoro Ortiz Tarrascusa/Alamy Stock Photo; (bottom right) (title page) nudiblue/Adobe Stock Photos; p. 18: The Book Worm/Alamy Stock Photo; p. 19: (bottom) (back cover) Howard Chew/Alamy Stock Photo; p. 21: Claus Lunau/Science Photo Library; p. 23: (top) Sandra Mu/Getty Images News/Getty Images; (bottom) Mark Pearson/Alamy Stock Photo; pp. 26, 27: Maxar/Getty Images; p. 28: Nature Picture Library/Alamy Stock Photo; p. 29: (top) Minden Pictures/Alamy Stock Photo; (bottom left) (Index page) Helmut Corneli/Alamy Stock Photo; (bottom right) Adisha Pramod/Alamy Stock Photo; p. 30: Philip Thurston/iStock/Getty Images.

NovaStar

ISBN 978 0 17 033510 2

Cengage Learning Australia
Level 5, 80 Dorcas Street
Southbank VIC 3006 Australia
Phone: 1300 790 853
Email: aust.nelsonprimary@cengage.com

For learning solutions, visit **cengage.com.au**

Printed in China by 1010 Printing International Ltd
1 2 3 4 5 6 7 29 28 27 26 25

Nelson acknowledges the Traditional Owners and Custodians of the lands of all First Nations Peoples. We pay respect to Elders past and present, and extend that respect to all First Nations Peoples today.

Contents

Ocean Exploration	4
Modern Mapping Methods	8
Geological Features on the Ocean Floor	14
Geological Activity on the Ocean Floor	22
Life on the Ocean Floor	28
Important Knowledge	30
Glossary	31
Index	32

Ocean Exploration

More than 70 per cent of Earth is covered by sea. While the planet's ocean is one huge, connected body of water, it is made up of five separate oceans: the Pacific, the Indian, the Southern, the Atlantic and the Arctic oceans.

The ocean is, on average, about 3500 metres deep, or about as deep as four Burj Khalifa towers stacked on top of each other. The shallowest spots are where the ocean meets land at beaches. Here, the sea may only be a few centimetres deep.

For thousands of years, people have been exploring these oceans, recording information about their coastlines and surrounding waters. First Nations peoples from Australia and the islands of the Pacific Ocean have used the stars and landmarks to help them **navigate** over water. They have passed this knowledge down through many **generations**, by telling and retelling the stories of their travels.

The Burj Khalifa in Dubai is the world's tallest building.

People have been exploring the oceans that cover most of the Earth for thousands of years.

In 1519, Portuguese explorer Ferdinand Magellan set sail with a fleet of five ships to find a route around the world. Although Magellan and many of his sailors died on the journey, one of the ships returned home with the first map of the **passage** around the continent of South America.

While maps of Earth's seas and continents are very detailed today, only about a quarter of the ocean floor has been mapped. In fact, the Moon's surface has been mapped more thoroughly than the ocean floor.

But knowing about the ocean floor and its **geological features** is important because it helps scientists to better understand how undersea activity affects weather patterns. This knowledge also helps to better predict changes to Earth's surface.

Droughts and floods can be caused by changes in the oceans, so understanding the oceans better helps people to prepare for weather extremes on land.

Measuring the Ocean's Depth over the Years

Knowing the ocean's depth was important to early explorers, and it still is today. Sailors need to know the depth of the water to prevent their ships from hitting underwater rocks or becoming **grounded** on the ocean floor.

More than 3000 years ago, Egyptians practised **bathymetry** to measure water depth. This involved pushing marked poles to the bottom of rivers and seas. In deeper water, sailors lowered ropes marked with measurements and a weight attached at one end, to gather more precise information. This process is called "sounding".

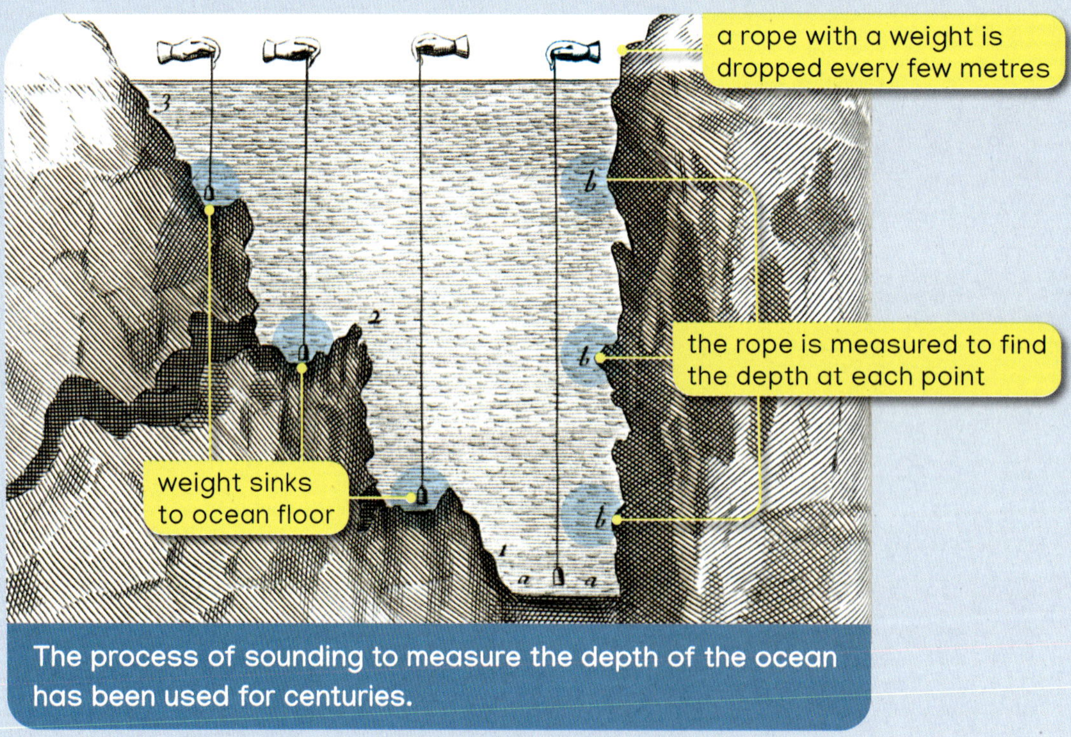

The process of sounding to measure the depth of the ocean has been used for centuries.

Sounding collected only a single measurement each time: the place where the weight landed on the sea floor. To add more detailed information to their maps, sailors had to measure the depth in multiple places. Joining the points of the same depth together on a map makes **contour lines**.

In 1872, British sailors and scientists aboard the HMS *Challenger* began the first global expedition to collect information about what was below the surface of the world's oceans. The scientists located the deepest place on Earth. Situated in the Pacific Ocean, this spot was named Challenger Deep, after their ship.

Information gathered by scientists on HMS *Challenger* produced the first comprehensive maps of ocean depth.

Ocean Zones

Scientists have divided the ocean beneath its surface into five separate zones. The names of the first three zones indicate the amount of light found in them.

The Zones of the Ocean

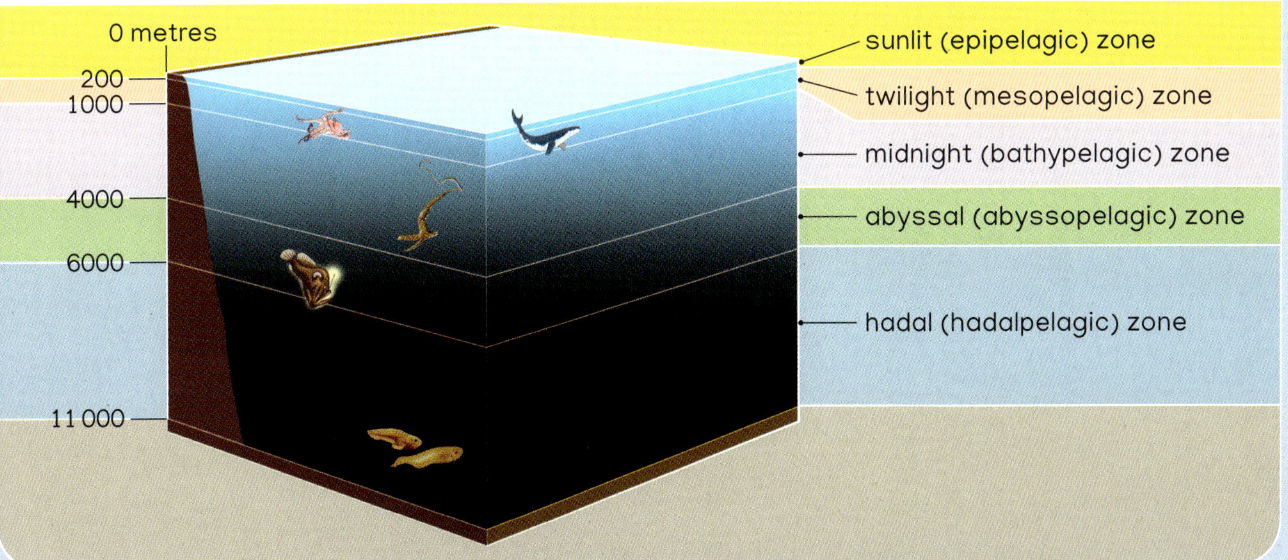

Hadal Zone

The hadal zone is named after Hades, the ancient Greek god of the underworld.

Modern Mapping Methods

Measuring ocean depths doesn't provide information about what objects are on the ocean floor or what they look like. But technology is helping scientists to learn more.

Sonar

A **sonar** device sends **sound waves** through water. When these sound waves hit solid objects, they are reflected back to the device, similar to how bats detect their food. The distances that are recorded allow scientists to create maps of the ocean floor.

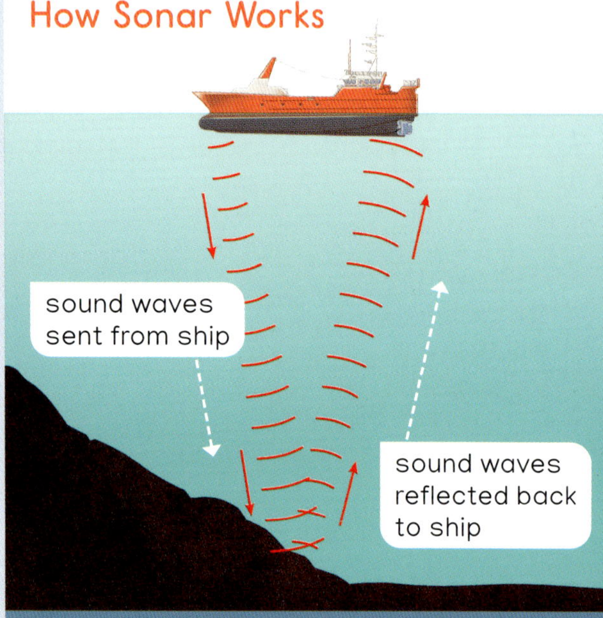

Sonar devices send and receive sound waves to detect how far away solid objects are.

Sonar is used by many boat owners to help with navigation.

Before sonar was invented in the early 1900s, most people believed the ocean floor was flat. In the 1950s, a geologist named Marie Tharp analysed information collected by sonar. She discovered that the ocean floor was, in fact, full of mountain ranges and valleys.

In 1977, Tharp and another geologist, Bruce Heezen, produced the first map that showed the **topography** of the world's ocean floor. Working with artist Heinrich Berann, they created a three-dimensional map that illustrated **terrain** such as underwater mountain ranges.

Marie Tharp, along with Bruce Heezen, created the first maps to show underwater mountains.

An Important Technology

The sinking of passenger liner RMS *Titanic* when it hit a part of an underwater iceberg in 1912 caused sonar technology to develop quickly. During World War I (1914–1918) and World War II (1939–1945), sonar became important in the hunt for enemy submarines.

The crew of a British nuclear submarine uses sonar technology.

Sonar and Tectonic Plates

Earth's solid crust is divided into seven major **tectonic plates** and many minor plates. Together, these plates are known as the **lithosphere**.

Movement in the **mantle** layer of Earth's core shifts the rocky plates. This movement constantly creates new crust and landforms on Earth.

Earth's Structure

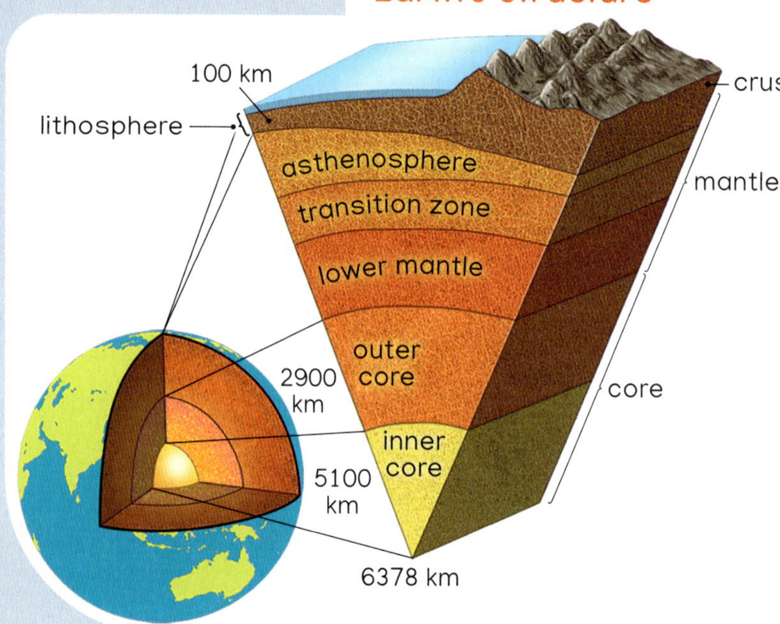

Boundaries of the World's Tectonic Plates

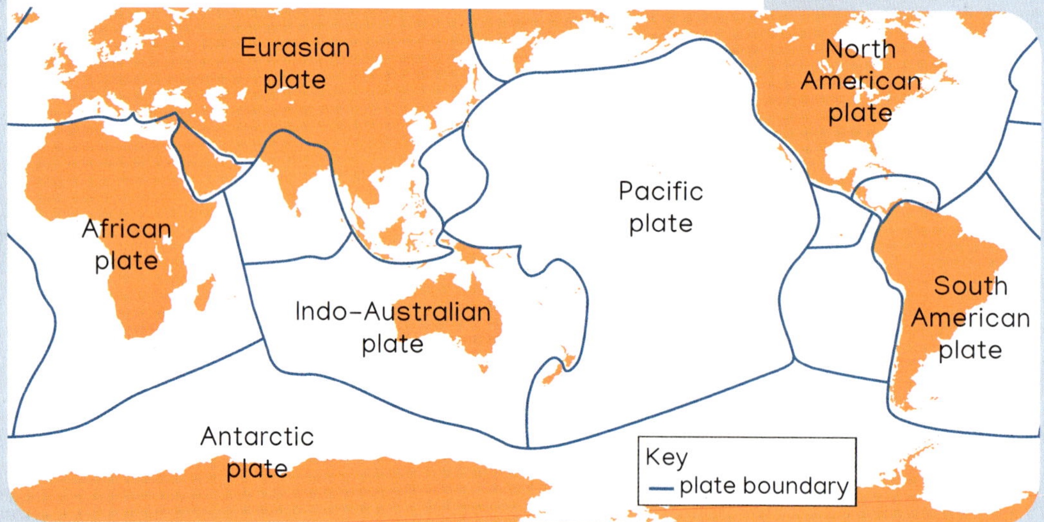

In the 1950s, Marie Tharp's use of sonar technology confirmed that Earth's crust was moving and changing. At the time, her findings were dismissed by other scientists. But modern sonar readings prove that tectonic plates can move between 2 and 15 centimetres each year. The places where plates "meet" are the most likely spots for earthquakes and volcanic activity.

Satellites and Radar

Sonar is used to measure distances and find objects below the surface of the ocean. Some satellites in orbit send **radar** signals towards a target on Earth. These signals travel through the air and the radio waves are reflected back to the satellite, similar to how sonar works. Computers calculate the distances the signals have travelled.

Radar signals are unable to travel through water very far, so they are used to measure the height of the ocean surface. The surface – the very top – of the ocean is not even, or level. The height of the surface changes, depending on what objects are below. For example, the surface of the ocean is higher over an underwater mountain and lower over an underwater **trench**. Scientists can use **data** from radar to build a picture of the ocean floor.

In the 1980s, scientist William Haxby created the first ocean floor map with satellite information and computers. His map showed new details of mountains, volcanoes and trenches.

Are Countries Washing Away?

It is important to know not just how deep the ocean is below its surface, but also how high the surface of the ocean is compared to land. The height of the surface can change, and the oceans are slowly becoming higher. Coastal communities around the world could be partly or entirely swallowed up by the sea if **climate change** causes this height to increase significantly.

Rising oceans are a threat to coastal communities.

Submarines, Submersibles and Remotely Operated Vehicles

Photographs, videos, soil samples and temperature readings from the bottom of the sea are important pieces of information used to create accurate ocean maps. But collecting this type of information can be risky and expensive.

Undersea exploration is dangerous because of pressure from the water. Pressure is the force of the water pushing on a person or object under the sea. The deeper below the surface, the more water pressure there is. This pressure limits how deep below the surface of the sea people can safely go.

Submarines are special vessels made to carry people underwater for long periods of time. They are constructed with strong materials, such as steel, so the pressure does not crush the **hull**. People are better protected in submarines. Some new submarines can go more than 2000 metres below the surface of the ocean.

An Australian Navy submarine can be at sea for 10 weeks with around 60 people on board.

Submersibles are vessels that spend only a short time underwater and must return to the surface for power or oxygen. There are several research submersibles that can reach 11 000 metres and carry up to two people. They can also carry cameras and other equipment. Trips in these submersibles are especially dangerous due to the high pressure on the hulls.

Remotely operated vehicles (ROVs) don't carry passengers. They have the ability to explore as deep as the ocean goes. They can be fitted with sonar and cameras and can be operated remotely, but ROVs are expensive.

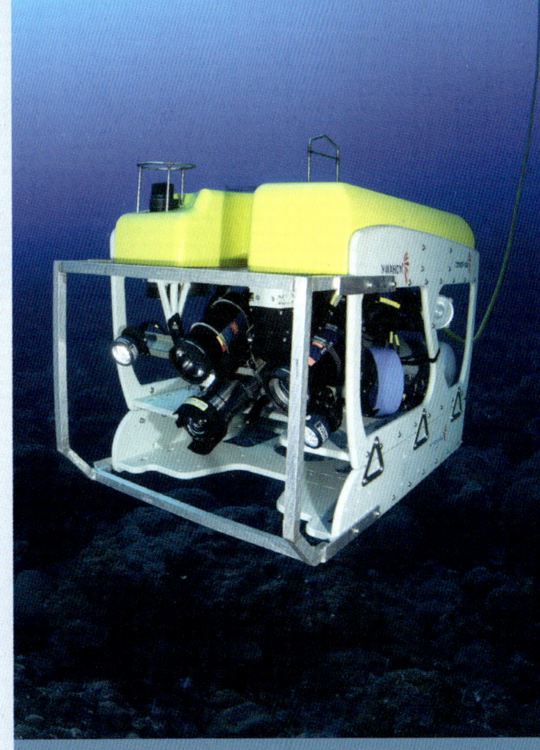

An Australian ROV is used for research in Antarctica.

Deepsea Challenger

In 2012, a deep-sea submersible built in Australia, the *Deepsea Challenger*, with one passenger reached the deepest recorded place on Earth, Challenge Deep (10 992 metres).

James Cameron, a film-maker, was the first person to travel to the bottom of the ocean in the *Deepsea Challenger*.

Geological Features on the Ocean Floor

Technology has helped expand people's understanding of the ocean floor and the types of geological features found at different depths.

Contintental Plates

Tectonic plates can be either continental or oceanic, depending on what is on top of them. The continental tectonic plates range in height from more than 8840 metres above the ocean surface to 3000 metres below water. Where a continental plate extends under the water, the geological formation is called a continental shelf. These shelves are generally flat with sandy or muddy bottoms. The water above is usually only a couple of hundred metres deep, or about the same measurement as a few cricket grounds laid out in a row.

Modern technology at work: crew members onboard a research ship use an ROV to explore the deep sea.

From the air, the change from the shallower continental shelf, under the paler water, to the darker, deeper water above the continental slope is clear.

The shelf ends in a continental slope. The slopes can be steep, and the water becomes suddenly quite deep, up to 3000 metres. This marks the end of the continent. The slopes are made up of soil **debris** that has come from the ends of rivers and coastal erosion that has hardened over time. The slopes can be smooth or have hills. They can also be cut into by underwater canyons that reach back into the continental shelf.

Geological Features of the Ocean Floor

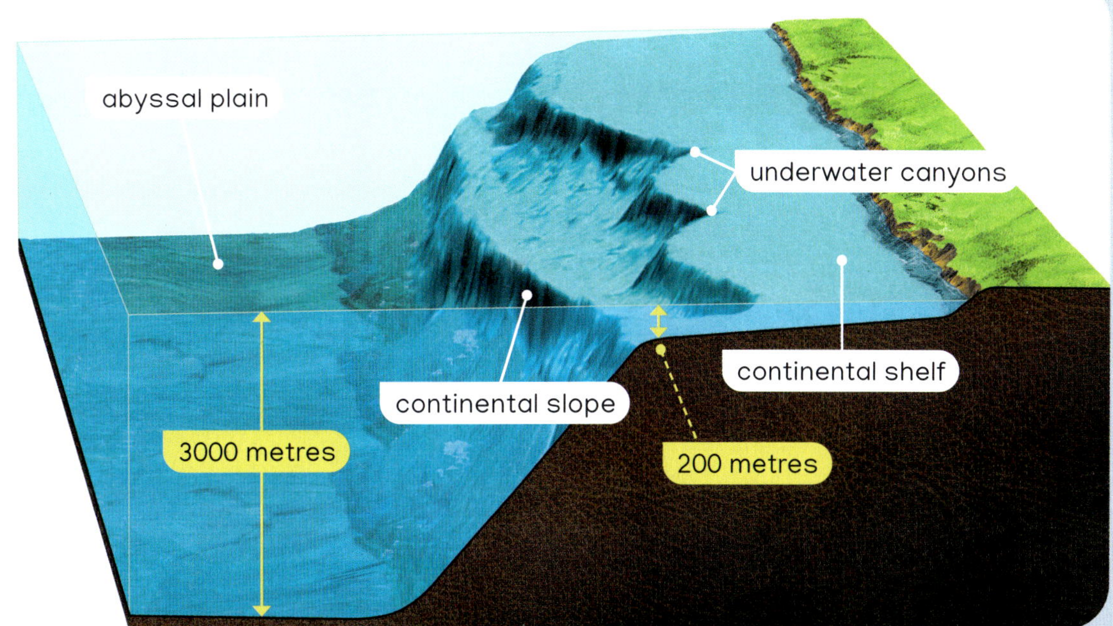

Mid-Ocean Ridges

Mid-ocean ridges are found on oceanic plates. Mid-ocean ridges are a series of underwater mountain ranges that extend 80 000 kilometres all around Earth's ocean floor. The ridges are found, on average, 2500 metres below the surface, but some are found much deeper. In some places they rise above the ocean surface.

Ridges are formed where the plates diverge, or move apart. When this happens, the hot, melted rock and other material is released from the mantle and makes new crust or new ocean floor. The speed of the moving plates affects the shape of the new land. Slower-moving plates create steeper land and taller underwater mountains than plates that move slightly more quickly.

Mid-ocean ridges – the most recently formed parts of tectonic plates – are shown in red on this map; areas in yellow, green and blue are older.

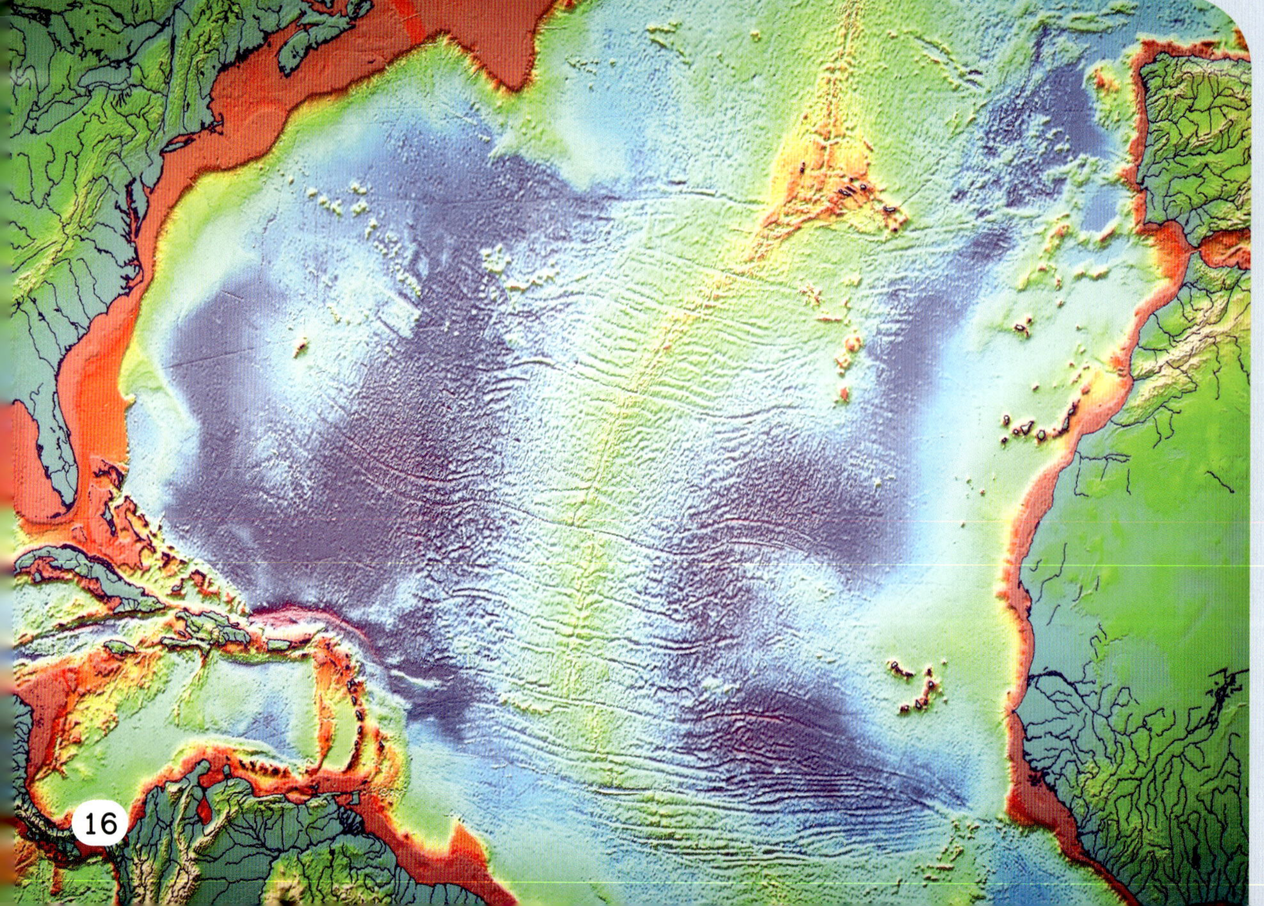

Walking on an Ocean Ridge

In places where the North American and Eurasian tectonic plates meet in Iceland, the Mid-Atlantic ocean ridge rises above the surface.

Where worlds collide: the boundary between tectonic plates is clear in Thingvellir National Park in Iceland.

People can walk – or even snorkel – between tectonic plates in Thingvellir National Park.

Abyssal Plains

Where the continental slopes end, they meet an abyssal plain. These flat plains are found between 3000 and 6000 metres below the ocean surface. They cover around 40 per cent of the ocean floor and are most plentiful in the Atlantic Ocean. The plains are covered in layers of the remains of ocean plants and animals, and grains of dirt from land erosion. Abyssal hills can rise from the plain and be as high as several hundred metres.

This is what the abyssal plain looks like – with light.

Seamounts

Seamounts are underwater mountains that rise from abyssal plains. Most are created by volcanic activity. They can be between 1000 and 4000 metres tall. While they are not high enough to break the ocean surface, some are very close. The Bowie Seamount in the Pacific Ocean comes within 24 metres of the surface, and the Vema Seamount near Cape Town, South Africa, has been measured just 21.5 metres below the surface.

Seamounts are plentiful with more than 10 000 already mapped. There are more to be discovered, with some scientists estimating there may be as many as 30 000.

Knowing a seamount's location is important, as it can help prevent ships from running aground on them.

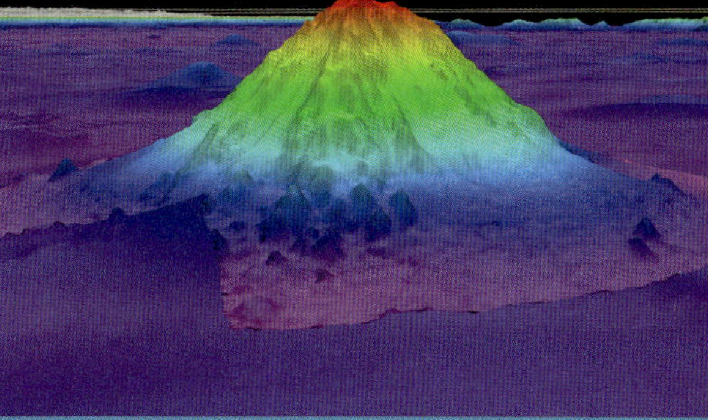

Seamounts, like this recently discovered one in the Pacific Ocean, rise dramatically from the abyssal plain.

Seamounts can sometimes be quite small.

The Great Meteor Tablemount

The Great Meteor Tablemount is a seamount in the North Atlantic Ocean. It is more than 4000 metres high and 110 kilometres around its base. That is similar to the average height of mountains in the Alps.

Trenches

Trenches are found in the deepest parts of the ocean, below 6000 metres. Trenches are long, narrow geological formations, similar to valleys. They form where two or more tectonic plates meet in a **subduction zone**. Most are found in the Pacific Ocean. As the heavier plate is pushed down and melts from the pressure and heat of the pushing, the melted material creates new mountains along the plate line, and the lighter plate is pushed upward. The narrow space between the two plates is the trench. Much is still unknown about these deepest places on Earth.

How Trenches are Formed

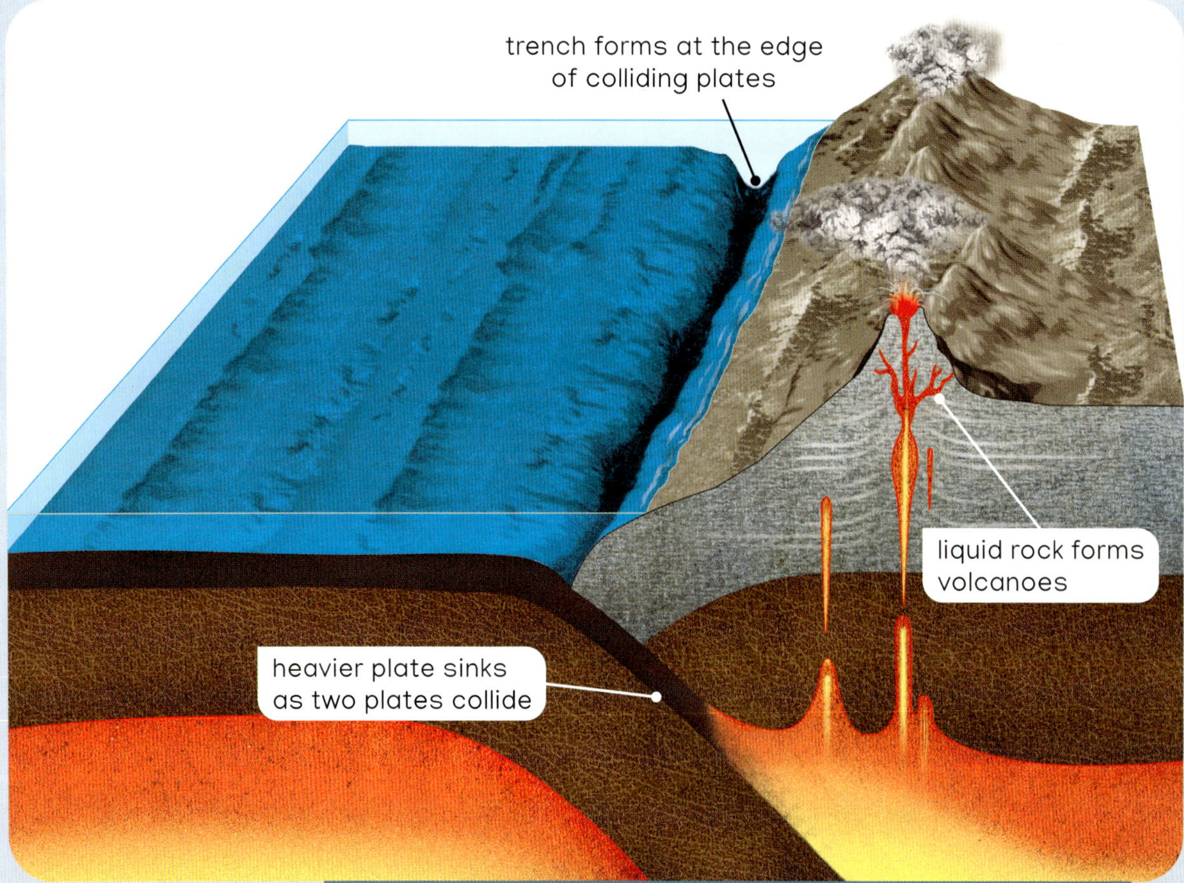

Ocean trenches are formed when tectonic plates collide.

The Mariana Trench

The world's deepest trench is the Mariana Trench in the western Pacific Ocean. Challenger Deep is the deepest point, measured at 10 994 metres below the surface of the ocean. It is deeper than Mount Everest, which measures 8849 metres, is tall.

This is how scientists imagine the Mariana Trench might look, if it had light.

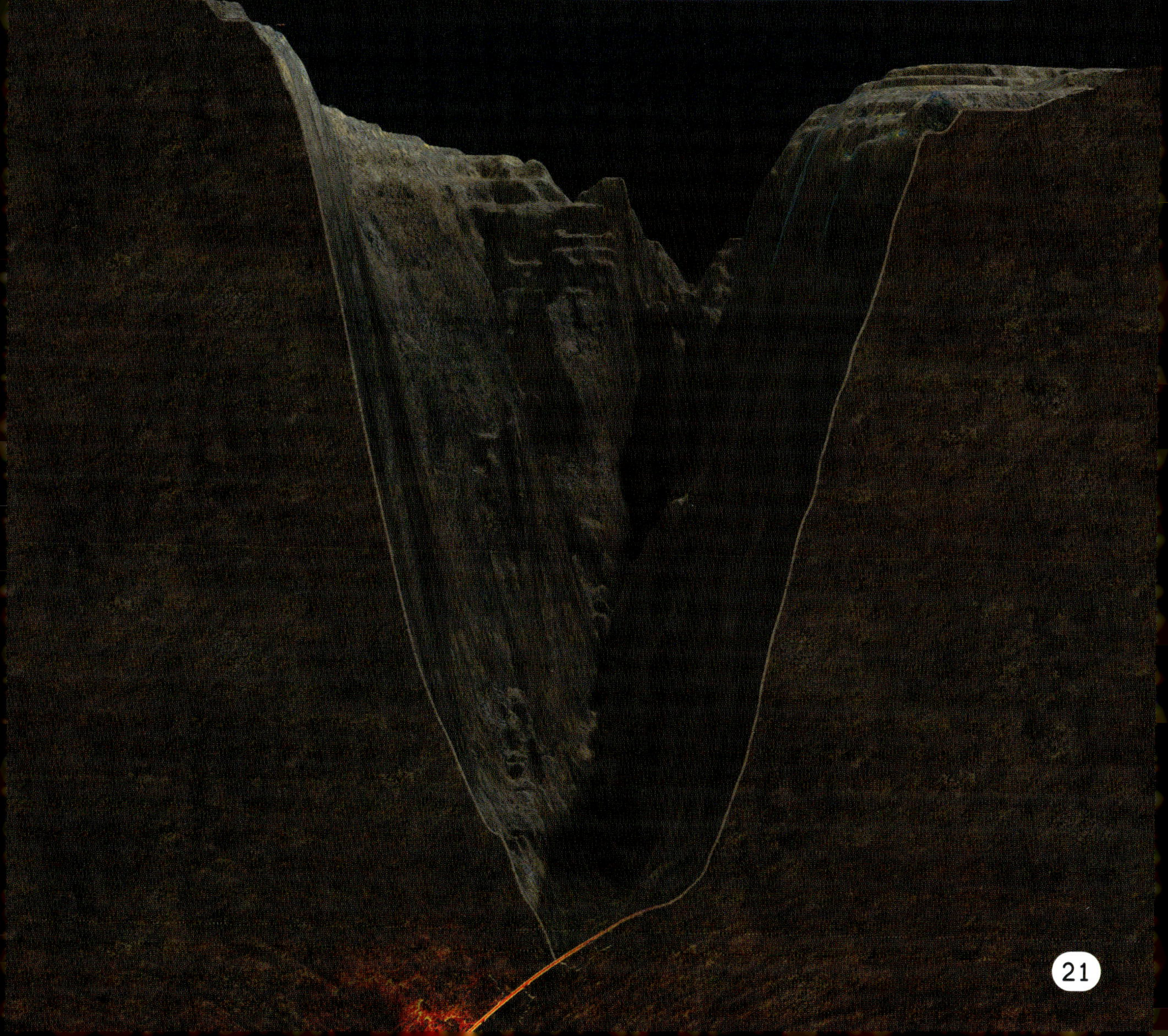

Geological Activity on the Ocean Floor

Underwater Earthquakes and Tsunamis

An earthquake is the shaking of the lithosphere. It is caused when two tectonic plates transform, or slip and bump against each other. There are about 55 earthquakes each day, both on land and under the ocean. An underwater earthquake can cause seamounts to break apart, crack open the ocean floor and send ripples of movement through the water. All of these events can cause a tsunami.

A tsunami is a series of giant surface waves. In the deep ocean, the waves may appear only half a metre high. As these waves roll towards shore, they gather speed and height. Since the Pacific Ocean has the most subduction zones and more tectonic plate movement than elsewhere, 80 per cent of tsunamis happen there. Tsunamis can reach speeds of more than 800 kilometres per hour, or as fast as a jet plane.

How a Tsunami Forms

A tsunami is caused by the energy from an earthquake.

In 2004, a massive earthquake, estimated at a **magnitude** of more than 9.0, occurred in the Indian Ocean. It was the most powerful ever recorded in Asia. It caused enormous tsunamis that reached 30 metres high – about the height of a 10-storey building. The waves reached far inland and, without any tsunami warning systems in place, they caused 230 000 deaths in fourteen different countries. Since then, countries have worked hard to create tsunami warning systems so that people will know when they should move inland to higher ground.

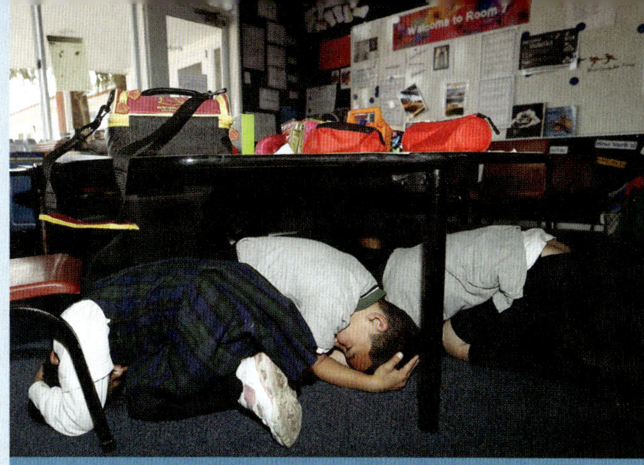
In New Zealand, earthquakes are common, and even children practise what to do in an earthquake.

The Indian Ocean tsunami in 2004 caused devastation in Indonesia.

Underwater Volcanoes

Along the mid-ocean ridges, underwater volcanoes are plentiful. Experts estimate there may be more than a million underwater volcanoes, most of them extinct. Underwater volcanoes take different forms, from cracks in the crust to cone-shaped mountains. Many volcanoes rise 1000 metres high from the seabed.

The most explosive volcanoes are found in subduction zones where tectonic plates converge, or move together. Here, a plate is pulled below another, melts and releases layers of molten material. Pressure builds under the layers until the molten rock breaks through and is released upward.

How a Volcano Forms in a Subduction Zone

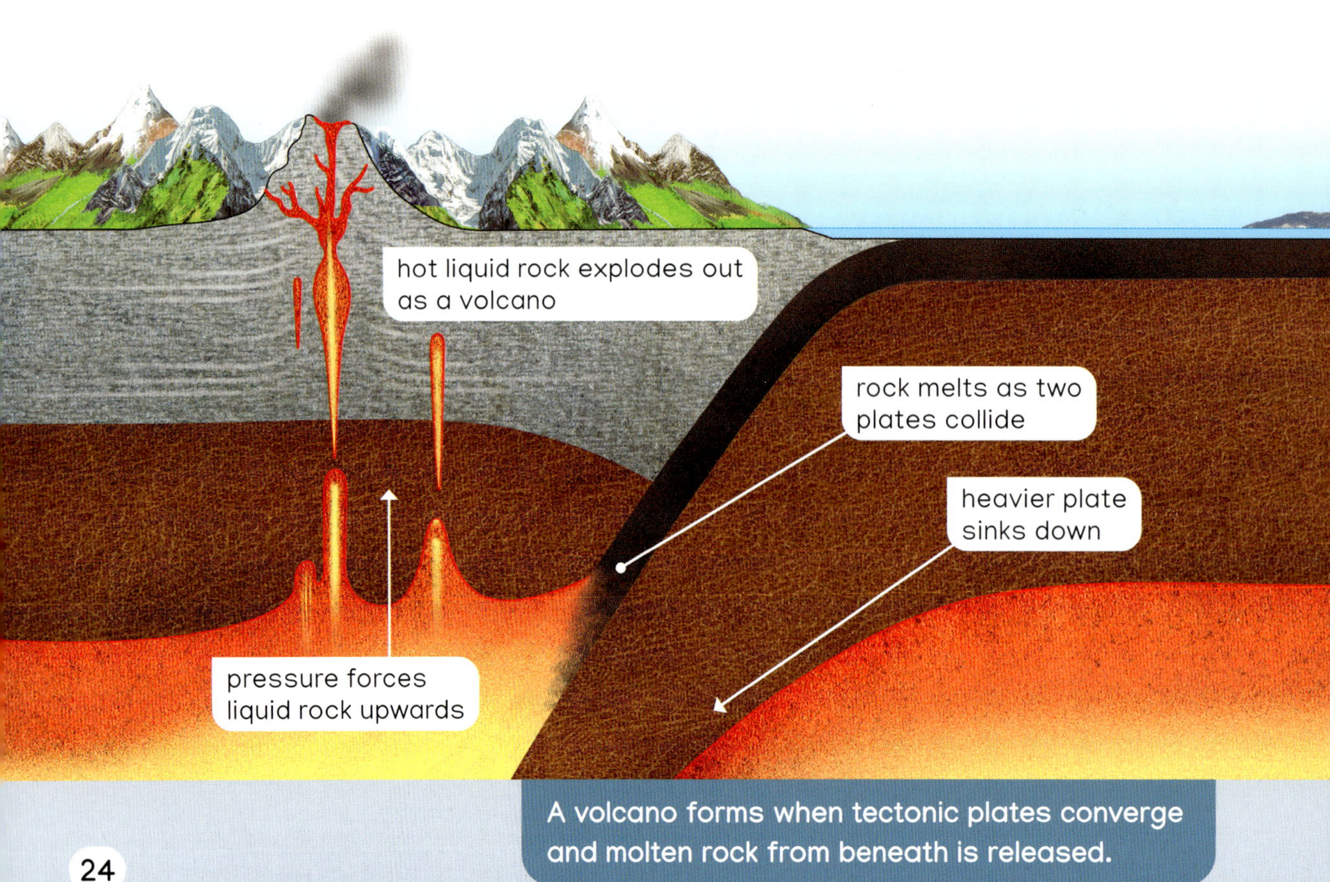

A volcano forms when tectonic plates converge and molten rock from beneath is released.

Other large volcanic eruptions can occur when an underwater volcano is on a "hot spot", an area where the Earth's crust is thin and the magma is closer to the surface. Mapping where a volcano is found and what type it is could help predict the size of eruptions.

Underwater volcanoes release ash, gases and molten rock from below Earth's crust. Most eruptions are not seen or noticed above the surface of the ocean.

Ring of Fire

The Ring of Fire is a 40 000-kilometre-long string of volcanoes that runs along the edge of the Pacific plate. About two-thirds of the world's volcanoes are found here, both on land and underwater.

The Ring of Fire and Tectonic Plates

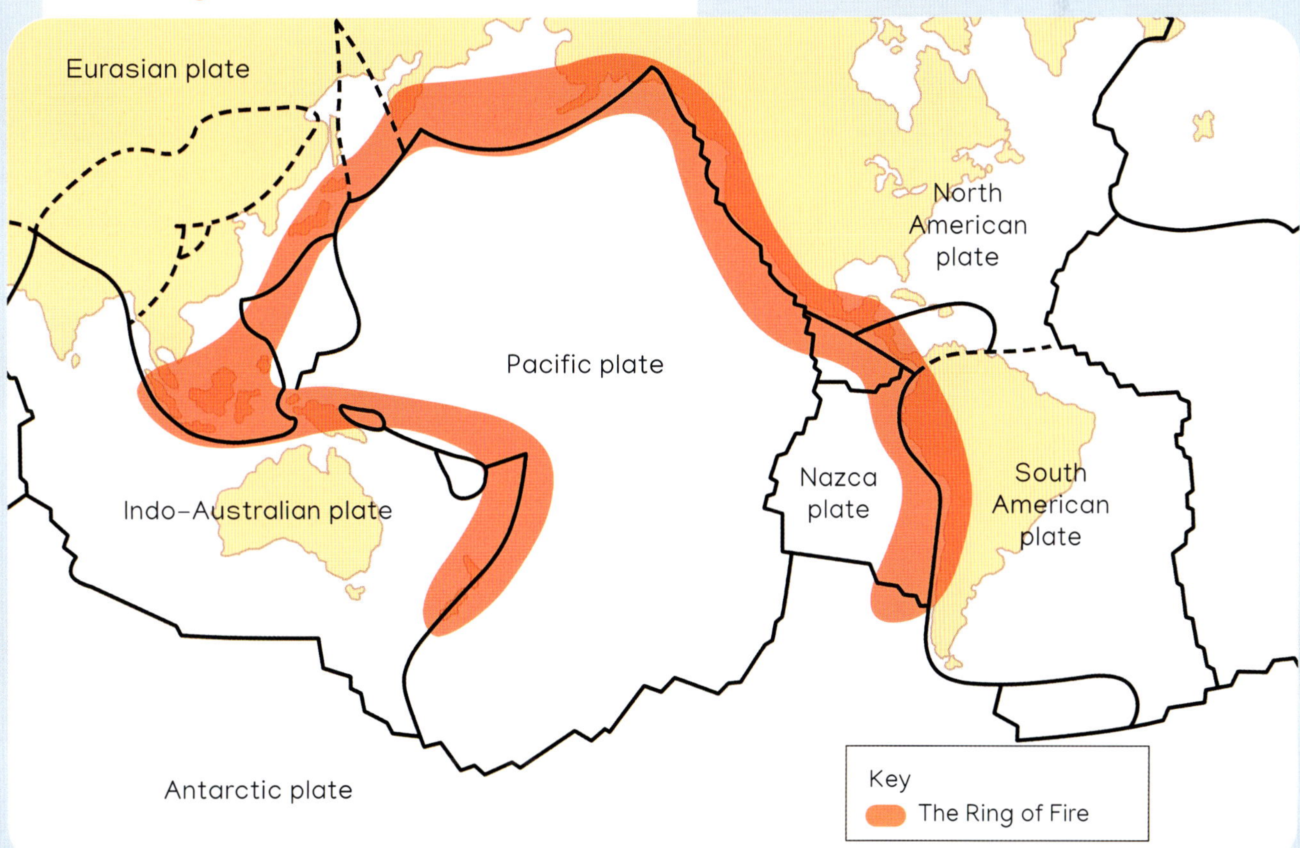

The Ring of Fire surrounds most of the Pacific Ocean and several major volcanoes and earthquakes have occurred here.

The Hunga Tonga–Hunga Ha'apai Volcano

The Hunga Tonga—Hunga Ha'apai volcano lies on the ocean floor between two islands in the South Pacific Ocean. It is in a subduction zone, between the Pacific plate and the Indo-Australian plate. There is evidence the volcano has been active for almost 1000 years. It has erupted several times since the 1900s.

In 2009 and again in 2015 it erupted and shot ash into the sky as high as 9 kilometres. These eruptions created new land, and expanded and joined the two uninhabited islands of Hunga Tonga and Hunga Ha'apai into one.

The volcano erupted again in December 2021. A month later, it erupted several times. The largest eruption, on 15 January 2022, shot vapour and ash 58 kilometres into the atmosphere. It was so large it could be seen from space.

These time-lapse images show the 2022 eruption as seen from space.

The explosion also released a sound wave that was heard two hours later in Aotearoa New Zealand and as far as Yukon, Canada, 9000 kilometres away. Much of the single island of Hunga-Tonga—Hunga Ha'apai was destroyed and ash covered nearby islands and reefs, killing plants and other living things.

Warming Earth

Almost 146 million tonnes of water were expelled into the air during the eruption of Hunga Tonga–Hunga Ha'apai. Scientists think this water vapour may remain in the atmosphere for a decade, trapping heat and leading to further warming of the planet.

The massive 2022 eruption shot ash 58 kilometres into the atmosphere.

Life on the Ocean Floor

Most marine life lives in the shallow waters of the sunlight zone. Some, like whales, may occasionally dive down deeper in search of food. But, as more advanced technology provides better ways to explore the deeper zones, scientists have been surprised to find new and strange forms of life.

Octopus and squid mostly live in the twilight zone. Whales will visit this zone in search of prey.

In the midnight zone, where there is no light, there are several species of fish that produce their own light, an ability known as bioluminescence. The pelican eel has an enormous mouth, giving it every chance to gobble up any food it might come across, while the end of its tail is able to glow pink.

Giant squid live in the midnight zone.

More bioluminescent marine life lives in the abyssal zone. The strange anglerfish has its own lamp sticking out on a stalk from its head.

Scientists from Western Australia helped discover the deepest fish ever recorded: snailfish, which were found more 8000 metres below the surface of the water in the hadal zone.

All these deepsea animals have evolved in extraordinary ways to survive where they do. As scientists learn more about them, they may be able to use this knowledge to improve people's lives.

Important Knowledge

Geological features under the surface of the ocean can cause movement that affects Earth's air and weather. This movement can also create new islands and destroy existing ones. Tsunamis that result from earthquakes under the water can endanger homes and habitats.

With so much of the ocean floor unexplored, the more data scientists can collect, the better the maps and animated models they can create. Mapping its seamounts, trenches and other geological forms can help to keep ships safe and to predict dangerous events, helping to save lives.

Understanding the ocean floor helps to predict dangerous events.

Glossary

bathymetry (*noun*)	from the Greek words for *deep* and *measure*, the science of measuring water depth
climate change (*noun*)	changes in the usual weather for a place or for the world
contour lines (*noun*)	lines on a map showing the measurement of the height of a landform or depth of water
data (*noun*)	information collected by observation or measurement
debris (*noun*)	small pieces left behind when something is destroyed
generations (*noun*)	groups of people who are born around the same time, usually within a range of 15 to 30 years
geological features (*noun*)	the details of the Earth's physical shape and structure
grounded (*adjective*)	when a boat is stuck on an underwater rock or the sea floor and cannot move
hull (*noun*)	the body of a ship or vessel that prevents water getting in
lithosphere (*noun*)	the Earth's outer layer
magnitude (*noun*)	the large size of something
mantle (*noun*)	the layer within the Earth between the crust and the outer core
navigate (*verb*)	to use tools or information to find your way
passage (*noun*)	a narrow space, such as a narrow waterway, allowing movement from one place to another around or between obstacles
radar (*noun*)	short for "radio detection and ranging"; a method to detect objects by sending out pulses of radio waves and measuring the distance and speed at which they are reflected back
sonar (*noun*)	short for "sound navigation and ranging"; a system to detect objects by sending out sound waves and measuring how long it takes for them to reflect back from an object once they hit it

sound waves (*noun*) waves of energy that travel from where sound is released

subduction zone (*noun*) where tectonic plates move together, or converge

tectonic plates (*noun*) the huge, slowly moving pieces that the Earth's outer layer is broken into

terrain (*noun*) the features and appearance of land: for example, rocky or sandy

topography (*noun*) the natural shape and physical features of land, such as mountains, cliffs and valleys, and their heights

trench (*noun*) deep cuts in the ocean floor, similar to valleys

Index

abyssal plain **18, 19**
Challenger Deep **7, 13, 21**
climate change **11, 31**
continental plates **14–15**
depth **4, 6, 7, 18**
earthquakes **10, 22, 23**
exploration **4–5, 12, 13, 14**
height, compared to land **11**
maps **5, 6, 8, 9, 11**
marine life **28–9**
measuring **6, 8**
mountains **8, 11, 16, 19, 22**
radar **11, 31**
sonar **8–9, 10, 11, 13 31**
subduction zone **20, 25, 32**
tectonic plates **10, 14–15, 16, 23, 25, 26, 32**
trenches **11, 20–1, 32**
tsunamis **22–3, 30**
volcanoes **10, 11, 24–6**
weather **5, 11, 30**
zones **7, 28–9**